The Adventures of Binder-Man

and how he changed his world (kind of)

The Adventures of Binder-Man
and how he changed his world (kind of)

Don Kuhl
Founder, The Change Companies®

Health Communications, Inc.
Deerfield Beach, Florida

www.hcibooks.com

**The Library of Congress Cataloging-in-Publication Data
is available through the Library of Congress**

© 2013 Don Kuhl

ISBN 13: 978-0-7573-1748-4 (paperback)
ISBN 10: 0-7573-1748-0 (paperback)
ISBN 13: 978-0-7573-1749-1 (epub)
ISBN 10: 0-7573-1749-9 (epub)

Publisher: Health Communications, Inc.
          3201 S.W. 15th Street
          Deerfield Beach, FL 33442-8190

Cover design by Jennifer Sande
Inside book formatting by Jennifer Sande

IT'S A BIRD!

IT'S A BIRD!

IT'S A PLANE!

IT'S A PLANE!

IT'S

IT'S...

...BINDER-MAN?

▸As mild-mannered Don Kuhl, I've had my fair share of failures.

I stuttered my way into the bottom half of my 1963 Lyons Township High School.

I flunked out of the University of Illinois in 1965.

I graduated first in my class of three in 1967 from The Hiram Scott College. The school closed in 1970.

I served as Director of Student Services at Midwestern College in 1968. It closed in 1970.

I served as Dean of Students at Tahoe Paradise College in California. It closed shortly after I left.

I started two statewide sports magazines, one in Colorado and one in Wisconsin. They both failed.

I received a Master of Science degree from Iowa State University. I worked in Student Administration for the University of Wisconsin System and as a Vice President of Business Development for a healthcare organization in the Midwest. (All of these institutions, thank goodness, are still in operation.) ▸▸▸

▶▶▶ And in 1989, I founded The Change Companies®, an organization dedicated to helping individuals make positive life changes.

But it was another few years before I finally learned to embrace life's challenges with good humor and some red spandex...

The year was 1993 and The Change Companies® (then called Serenity Support Services) was at a crossroads. In our fifth year of existence, much of everyone's time was spent filling orders for Interactive Journals, our trademark printed product, by putting sheets into three-ring binders. Our tiny staff couldn't keep up with the demand, and money was tight.

I had created this company with the goal of putting the research of behavior change directly into the hands of the end user. Our Interactive Journals would eventually go on to serve nearly 4,000 agencies and corporations worldwide and assist over 20 million people, but back then, small business struggles and the sheer time it took to fill each order of three-ring binders seemed overwhelming.

During these periods of angst and insecurity appeared Binder-Man, a superhero of softening flesh and very common superpowers. I created this character to bring a little joy and humor to the otherwise banal task of binder-filling.

The occasional costume change that took me from struggling business owner to silly, blue-and-red-clad superhero is what saved The Change Companies®. With his flowing red cape and matching earmuffs and slippers, Binder-Man proclaimed to our loyal employees, nearby businesses, and gawking passersby that our organization was here to stay.

Ever since that time, I have been reminded that it's the little choices we make each day that keep an individual, or an organization, moving in the right direction. The Change Companies® is built on this core belief. I continue to be blessed with employees who blend their skills, passion and personalities into their work, and we grow more dynamic through the choices and changes we encounter each day.

Binder-Man doesn't make too many appearances anymore, but his adventures extend well beyond his caped-crusading days. This collection of personal stories represents some of the lessons about change I have learned, failed to learn, or am still in the process of learning.

Whether it be a behavior change or costume change, I believe there is a superhero within all of us who can do battle with the forces of fear, inertia, and self-doubt. This inner power reveals itself whenever we are confronted with personal or professional peril. It's a privilege to share these adventures with you. ■

TABLE OF CONTENTS

TABLE OF CONTENTS

To Sherry

Thanks for the hike.

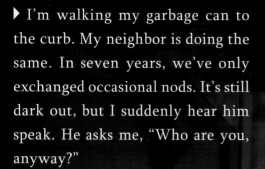

▶ I'm walking my garbage can to the curb. My neighbor is doing the same. In seven years, we've only exchanged occasional nods. It's still dark out, but I suddenly hear him speak. He asks me, "Who are you, anyway?"

Is he being rude or just curious? Either way, I figure his question deserves an answer, so I stand next to my garbage thinking of an appropriate response.

Is he wondering about my job? About my family? Do my past or current circumstances really define who I am? Somehow, none of this seems to be what he's asking about.

Maybe he wants to know about my core beliefs, what I really care about. After all, aren't the beliefs we accumulate over a lifetime, and the way they cause us to feel and act, the most representative feature of who we are? ▶ ▶ ▶

RP02 050444

▶▶▶ Tired of my silent self-reflection, my neighbor starts walking back to his house. I feel my time for a satisfying response running out. This could be the start of a meaningful friendship.

"My name is Don," I call out in the dark.

I hear nothing back. My neighbor is already at his door.

As I slowly head inside, I have several thoughts on my mind:

He was just being friendly and I blew an opportunity.

The tendency to overthink things can undermine an otherwise simple answer.

I still don't know his name.

And just who am I, anyway? ■

And just who am I, anyway?

COMMANDS

▶ My German shepherds rarely follow my instructions. Simple orders such as "don't chase the cat" or "bring me the newspaper" are ignored. No matter how rational or well-presented my commands might be, I get nothing but blank stares. Now that I think of it, trying to command behavior change has never gotten me very far either.

When my son and daughter were younger, I attempted to discipline them in a similar way. I would enforce household rules by pointing out behavior defects and trying to command compliance. Anyone who's interacted with teenagers will recognize that this approach is an exercise in futility.

There have been other times where I felt it appropriate to tell friends they "must" stop smoking or "should" lose weight. While these friends were kind enough to refrain from calling me self-righteous to my face, I certainly didn't move them along the path to healthier living.

So if my personal approaches to behavior change have been less than ideal, what does work? ▶ ▶ ▶

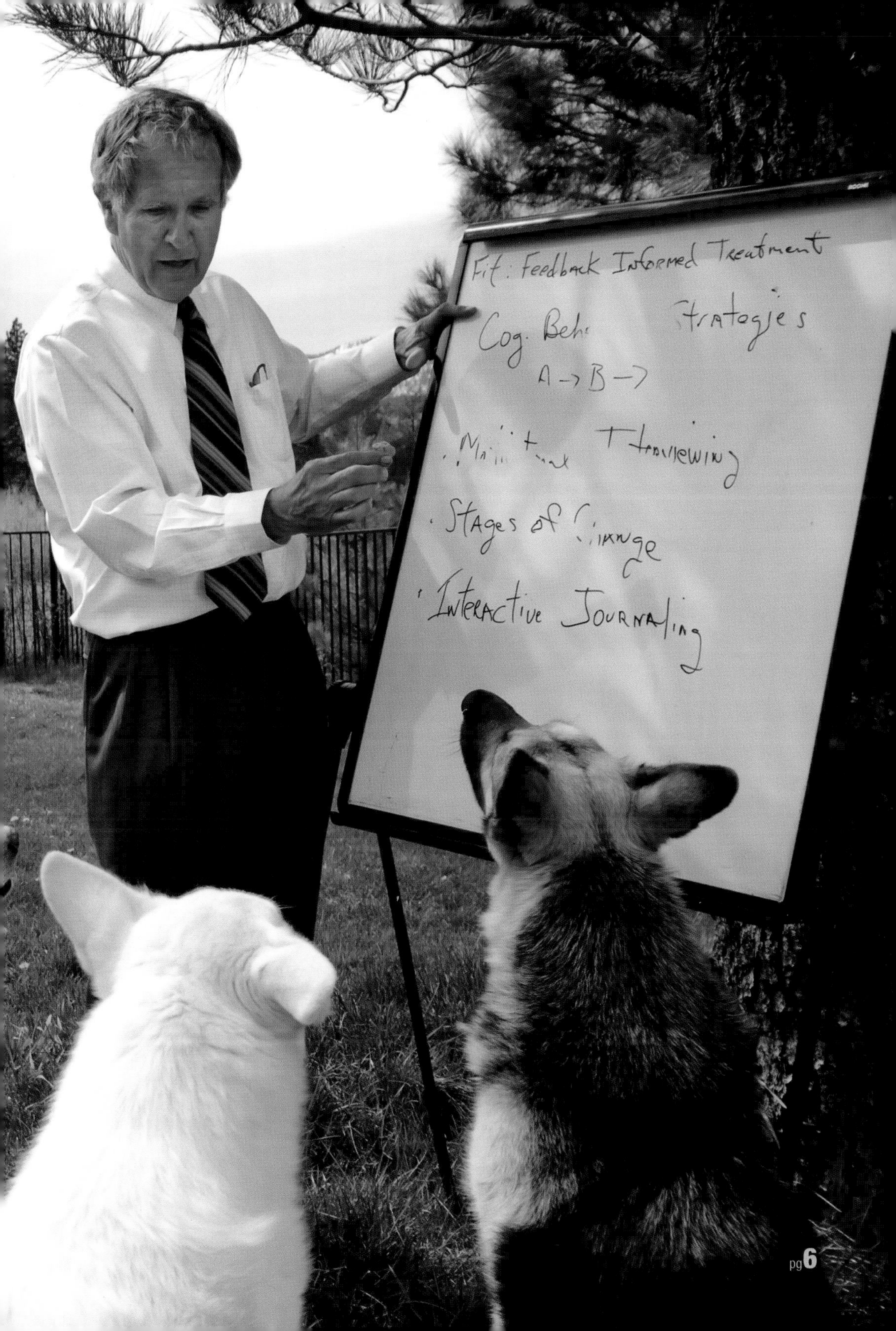
Fit: Feedback Informed Treatment
Interactive Journaling

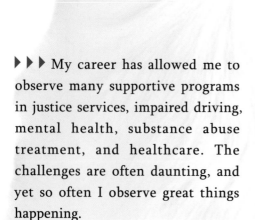

▶ ▶ ▶ My career has allowed me to observe many supportive programs in justice services, impaired driving, mental health, substance abuse treatment, and healthcare. The challenges are often daunting, and yet so often I observe great things happening.

No one can push or direct another person toward behavior change. Those who are offering support to someone during a life change succeed by walking alongside that individual. They show respect, compassion, and confidence.

Why am I so slow in applying these proven strategies to my personal life? Even today, my adult children chuckle when I lecture them on money management, my friends mock my "words of wisdom," and my German shepherds continue to chase the cat.

Instead of sticking with my instructional approach, I'm going to follow the example of those people in my life who support me through troubled times. Through their gentle guidance, they help me tap into my own strengths and resources along the way to positive change. ■

My adult children chuckle when I lecture them on money management, my friends mock my "words of wisdom," and my German shepherds continue to chase the cat.

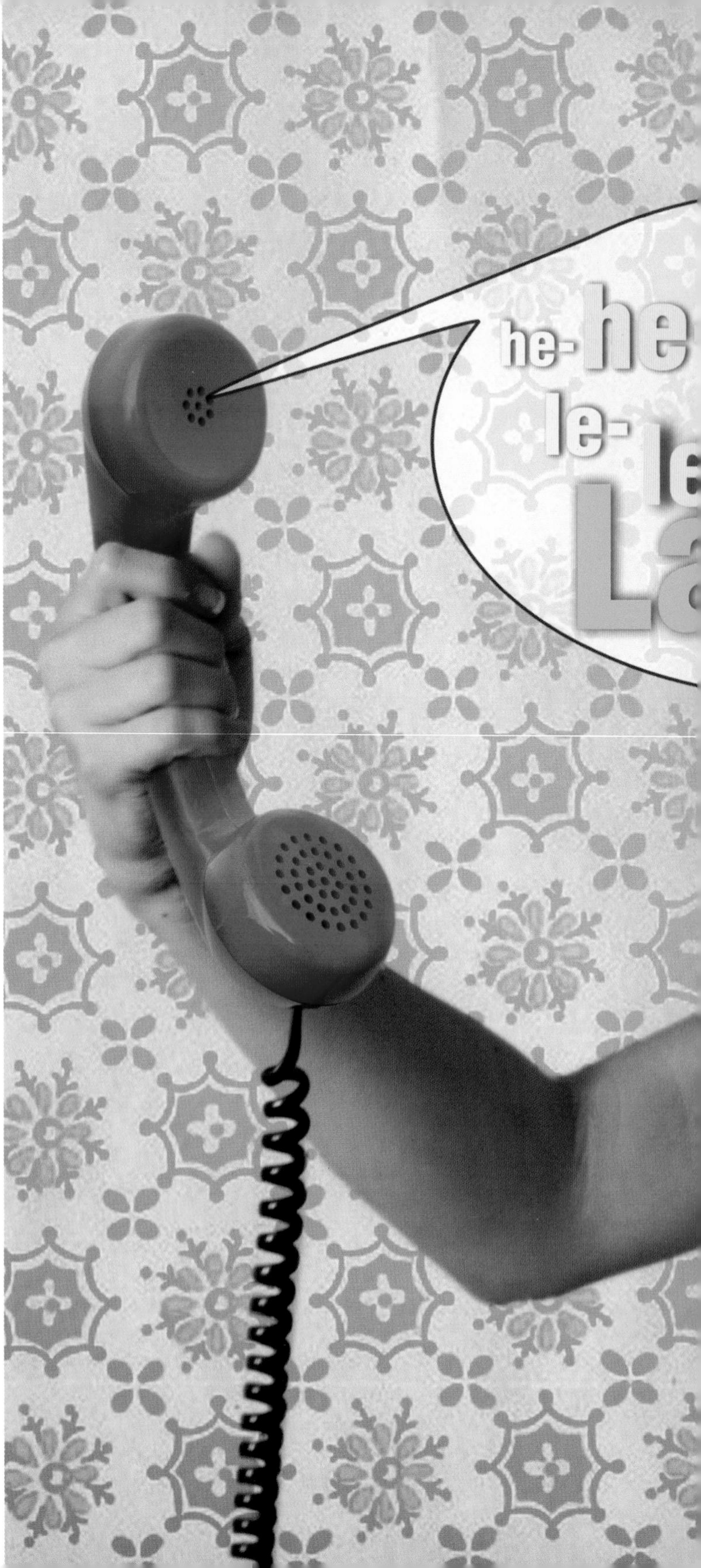
he-he
le-le
La

▶ Tough situations for a child stutterer: quarterbacking a team without receiving a delay of game penalty; trying to smile at stuttering jokes; attempting to roll my Rs in Spanish class; calling the popular Lana Thorpe to ask her to the school dance.

My father and other well-meaning people kept telling me to think about what I wanted to say before I started talking. I always knew what I wanted to say. I just couldn't get the darn words out of my mouth.

Then a college professor, Frank Tate, encouraged me to stutter on purpose. This simple tip turned the tables. I had power over my impediment. I became responsible and in charge of my behavior.

Delightfully, I chose my "payback" to former tormentors by purposefully injecting a stammer or two and watching their impatience fester.

In retrospect, my stutter has been a blessing in disguise. It taught me to be sensitive to the challenges facing others. I found a love of reading and writing on my own. I talked less and listened more, although I'm still working on that one.

My stutter also revealed a broader lesson for me to consider. When I encounter circumstances that appear to be disastrous or insurmountable, I pay attention to my ongoing "self-talk." I allow this inner voice to help me understand the issue at hand and consider various ways to move forward. This allows me to be the "owner" of the circumstance; I am in charge of the outcome.

I'm not talking about putting on a pair of rose-colored glasses. Often, success is derived from taking ownership of a personal challenge or problem and then making courageous, tiny decisions each day. Faced with the same negative circumstances, one person's self-talk could be about being a defeated victim, while another uses the situation as a springboard for emotional development and new possibilities.

I c-could never have ta-taken Lana Thorpe to the dance if I hadn't picked up the phone. ■

Oh no, oh no, domino!

oh no, domino!

▶ President Dwight D. Eisenhower first coined the phrase "domino effect" to apply to the spread of Communism in the 1950s. Although the stakes may not be as high, my international eating and television viewing habits seem to follow the same domino effect that threatened the free world.

My week starts with a bite of Bavarian cheesecake. This small transgression tumbles into a German chocolate cake after I had already surrendered my defenses to French fries and Swedish meatballs. Before I even have a chance to unfold the morning's paper, the dangerous spread of sweets and treats has invaded my entire continental self.

This same domino effect has influenced how I watch TV. It started as a pleasant investment of an hour per week with Mark Harmon and NCIS. Then, a brief reconnaissance mission informed me that NCIS reruns could be found on other channels every day of the week. Soon, my attention to less glamorous activities, such as house maintenance and personal grooming, gave way to this new, time-consuming opportunity. I eventually found a whole batch of new television dramas that combine humorous banter, dissection of corpses, and deadly gunfights.

Fortunately, the same domino effect can work in reverse. For example, I started yesterday morning with a carrot stick, then a juicy orange at lunch. These led me to a fruit smoothie after work. My healthy decisions dominoed into a dinner of steamed broccoli over long-grain brown rice and a trip to the grocery store to purchase green vegetables I can't even pronounce.

In the world of behavior change, it is understood that a small, positive action can lead to multiple behaviors of a similar kind. All it takes is a gentle shift in one direction to start a chain reaction leading to significant progress.

What a wonderful realization. So today, when I consider getting more exercise, I don't need to sign a nine-year contract at Hardbodies Forever Fitness. All I need to do is lace up my tennis shoes and begin walking down Carson Street. My path will take me along those big aspen trees and right by…Donuts To Go.

Oh no, domino! ■

FLUNKED

UNIVERSITY OF ILLINOIS
VERY OFFICIAL DOCUMENT

Dear Donald,

YOU FLUNKED OUT, YOU LOSER!

OUT.

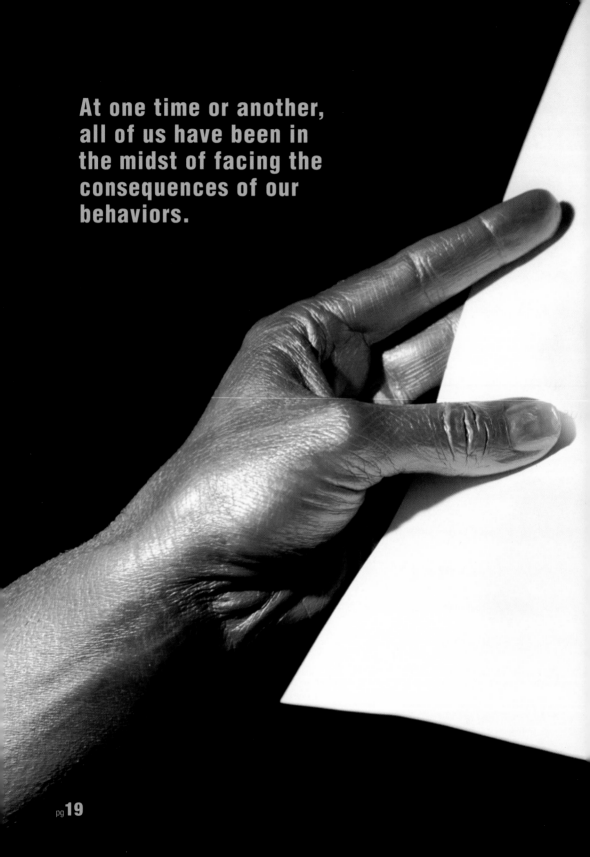

At one time or another, all of us have been in the midst of facing the consequences of our behaviors.

▷ It's 1964 and I'm sitting alone in the back row of a theater in Urbana, Illinois. Shirley Bassey is singing Goldfinger and shimmering images of golden women dance across the screen. I have a beer in one hand, a box of popcorn in the other, and a formal letter from the University of Illinois tucked in my back pocket informing me I have just flunked out of school. I'm afraid, embarrassed, and I may be crying.

A few years later, I'm hitchhiking across Nebraska. A rusted Ford Fairlane stops, and even as I hop in the back, I know it's the wrong ride. A young man and older woman are in the front. Between them on the seat are a handgun, a half-empty bottle of Jim Beam, and a cowboy hat. I slide in next to a skinny boy picking his fingernails with a pocketknife. Eighty miles later, near Ogallala, the car slows and I'm tossed into a ditch, bleeding and naked.

A few more years pass. Over 40 men are packed in the cell at the Maricopa County Jail in Phoenix. They all look tougher and older than I am. Feeling like an imposter, I try to blend in. A stocky, bald man with huge arms walks over to me, smiles, and spits in my face. I look down as if I've dropped something on the ground and slowly back away.

Nearly four decades have passed but I still recognize these events as defining moments that eventually moved me toward sanity, responsibility, and joy.

At one time or another, all of us have been in the midst of facing the consequences of our behaviors. The weight of change falls on each individual. Thankfully, though, difficult circumstances can be converted into starting points for healthy decisions and constructive actions.

The ex-student in the Urbana theater, the naked kid along old Highway 80, and the young man in a Phoenix jail are all grateful that change is possible. ■

HOW BIG IS

YOUR GOLF CUP?

My friend Mike Hooper has never missed a short putt in his life. Every time I hear the "clink" of his ball in the cup, I curse under my breath.

Mike doesn't pay attention to the slope of the green or the cut of the grass. He simply pictures his tiny golf ball going into a huge cup. Mike, along with many other successful people I know, understands that his beliefs and assumptions affect how his personal and professional life unfolds.

Dr. Bill Miller explains that who and what we think we are guides the choices and behaviors we make each day. What we believe to be true directly influences the outcomes we experience.

In response to an individual looking for different outcomes, Miller asks the following questions:

Are you basically a worthwhile and lovable person?

How able are you to change?

Who's in charge of your life?

Do you see your shortcomings as temporary setbacks from which to learn and change?

How do you describe yourself?

When I think of Mike Hooper, I want to add a question of my own to Miller's list:

How big is your golf ball cup?

The assumptions we live with on a daily basis may feel indisputable, but they can be changed. When I "live as if" I possess certain qualities (such as humility, compassion, or confidence), my thoughts, feelings, and actions begin to follow suit.

Yesterday, my golf ball was only 26 inches from the cup. I had a chance to save a bogey on the first hole. I thought of Mike Hooper. I thought about the person I wanted to be.

"Clink." ∎

BUCK UP.

▶ Willie Wilkerson was a real whiner. He wouldn't last a day at The Change Companies®, where we've posted a corporate sign promoting a unique solution to life's challenges. It says: "Buck up. Eat a banana. Walk around the block." This message certainly could have helped my friend Willie. He always felt ignored and underappreciated. He schlepped through life under a dark cloud of self-pity.

I knew Willie back when I hung out at a local bar named Lucky's. Everyone who wasn't lucky used to meet there after work to feed off of each other's narcissistic pessimism. Willie's specialty was being a victim of his boss, his wife, his neighbor, and a wide range of local, state, and federal government agencies.

Nothing was Willie's fault. When it came to action, he was always a nitpicking spectator. Willie could spend two hours and five beers describing why parking meters were constitutionally illegal and how his aging collection of tickets served as a symbol of his patriotism. "Why don't all of us fill these damned envelopes with cat poop and mail them to the mayor?" Willie shouted to the rest of us sitting on barstools.

Today, I think of how Willie stacks up against our corporate sign. It's just a few phrases strung together, but it represents some clear alternatives for life's choices.

As individuals, we can choose to either buck up or keep complaining.

We can either eat a banana or drink another beer.

We can either walk around the block or twirl dizzily on a barstool.

Whenever I feel like giving up on a worthy challenge, I think of Willie Wilkerson while I'm lacing up my red high-tops. ■

▶ My ears are growing like cucumbers. I can't seem to stop them. And my nose is following suit.

My lengthening ears and prominent nose are partly a factor of genetics and partly a factor of age, neither of which is something I have control over. Nevertheless, whenever I study my face in the mirror, I see a grotesque caricature of my former self staring back at me. What happened to that confident guy I used to be, so sure of his "special look"?

To my rescue comes Reinhold Niebuhr's Serenity Prayer. Through this simple prayer, millions of individuals have learned to accept the things they cannot change, find the courage to change the things they can, and have the wisdom to know the difference.

When I recite Niebuhr's Prayer, I remember that I cannot change my genes, just like I cannot stop myself from aging. Whenever I reflect on my reflection, I know I'm learning to accept the self I continue to become. My ears aren't getting any smaller, but that confident guy in the mirror is returning. ■

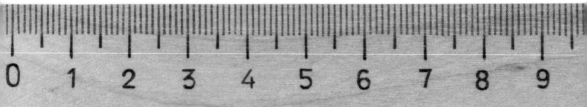

I'm learning to accept the

self I continue to become.

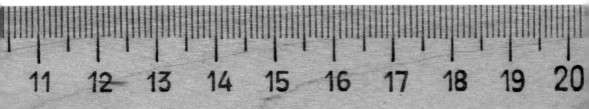

It's a different era today, with different kinds of heroes than when I was growing up. Even still, I hope my grandsons find a Mr. Hogan of their own.

When I was a child, there was a police officer assigned to watch our neighborhood. His name was Mr. Hogan, but when he wasn't within hearing range, all the kids called him Hopper Copper. The story went that he caught an artillery shell right in his butt during the last day of action in WWII. As a result, he limped when he walked and hopped when he ran.

Us neighborhood boys did little things to keep Hopper Copper on the run. It wasn't anything really bad. Our parents called them "punishable pranks," but we called them by colors and numbers like football plays. For example, "Green 42" was swiping Christmas lights from one neighbor's yard and decorating the yard across the street. "Red 33" was toilet papering the houses of girls in our seventh grade and putting strawberry jelly in their mailboxes.

Bobby Easton was the fastest kid in our school. Whenever Hopper Copper chased us, Bobby would slow down and fall behind the rest of us less athletic boys. He would turn off down a different road, with Hopper Copper right at his heels. Then, when we were a safe distance away, Bobby would take off at full speed and the chase would be over. ▶▶▶

I never thanked Hopper Copper for putting up with us, but he's the type of hero I hope everyone has the chance to experience.

▶ ▶ ▶ Of course, Mr. Hogan knew who we were and knew our parents. If we ever got too out of line, he would come over for a friendly visit. He would always say we were good kids at heart, but he also knew our dads would take us down to the basement for a real spanking after he left.

Our favorite evenings were playing basketball under the lights at Brookside Park. We'd shovel the snow or play in the rain. There was something special about those nights. It was as if huge crowds were watching us when there was actually only one fan: Hopper Copper. The park lights were metered and it cost a dime an hour to keep playing. Hopper Copper would stand by the light pole with his arms crossed. When one of us made a great play, he'd give us three big claps. After an hour, the lights would make a soft pop and then slowly fade. The players would rush over to Hopper Copper and beg him to put another dime in the meter. He always had a dime and always lit up our court.

I never thanked Hopper Copper for putting up with us, but he's the type of hero I hope everyone has the chance to experience. ■

▶ If you could go back in time and change one personal behavior that affected your relationships with others, what would it be? For me, I wish I'd granted more wiggle room to my family, friends, and fellow workers.

Over my lifetime, I've expected others to give me all kinds of wiggle room. I've frittered away countless hours, made many ill-advised choices, and fruitlessly attempted to disguise my failures as victories, all the while asking that those around me accept my shortcomings.

Yet, I always expected my children to toe the line and perform great feats with no lapses. When they slacked off, I was all over them with fear-provoking facial frowns and a list of corrective measures to put them back on track. Likewise, when I thought my friends' behavior had not measured up to my standards, I would chastise them through "character-building sarcasm."

And I saved the most egregious expectations for employees. Gifted people would be doing great work. Passion would be in the air. Jobs would be getting done. Still, I would surmise that someone must have been slacking off, not working to capacity. Would a truly dedicated employee squander his whole lunch break actually eating lunch? Should weekends consist of two full days in a row without accomplishing any work?

I wish I hadn't wrapped people up so tightly with my expectations, and had given them as much wiggle room as I demanded from others. I could have encouraged my friends to bask in an important moment or task, even when it caused them to be late for dinner. When my kids spilled ice cream on their Sunday clothes, I could have made them laugh instead of fret. And, if an employee's favorite team was playing at home, I could have made him feel guiltless when he called in with a mild case of the flu.

Of course, none of us can go back and alter the past, but the joy of life is that we can begin to change our thoughts, beliefs, and behaviors at any time we choose. So, as of today, I will not wrap people up so tightly. I will grant people more space to create their own victories and mistakes. I declare more wiggle room for everyone. ■

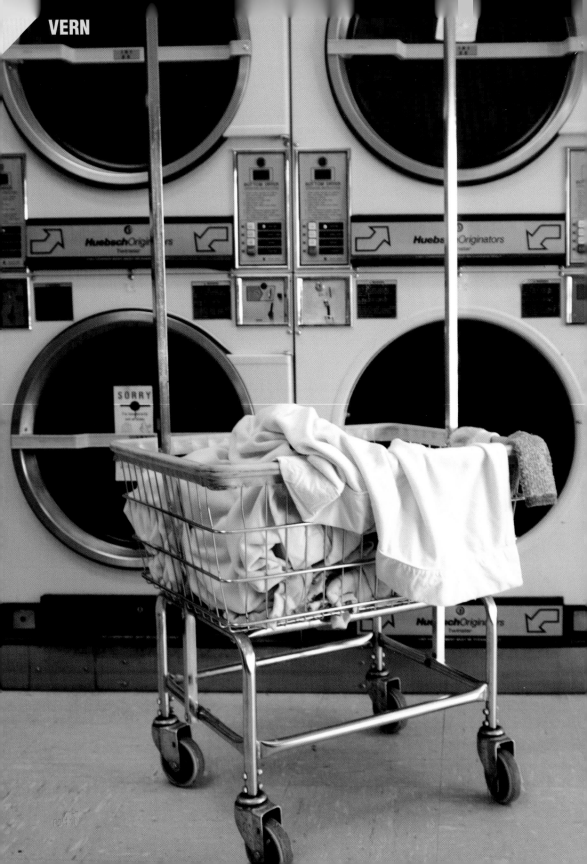

It's never too late to be blessed with a loving relationship.

▶ I wonder how often I have allowed personal traumas or difficult circumstances to keep me from experiencing the love of those I'm most connected to. Before he died on September 26, 1999, my dad helped me understand that it's never too late to let a loving relationship into my life.

Vern was born in Ogden, Iowa. Over the years, he took jobs as a soldier, a bank teller, a bookkeeper, and a salesman. He married Irene and fathered four children. I was the youngest.

Growing up, we rarely connected. During my school years, he crisscrossed the Midwest selling grain storage equipment. He would return home on occasional weekends with his left arm berry-brown from the sun and state maps filling the locked glove compartment of his car.

Irene always paired the two of us up to do the wash at a laundromat around the corner. I'm uncertain which of us she was punishing. As a high school freshman, I leaned away from the laundromat's dirty windows so as not to be seen by the popular kids. Vern sweated profusely just waiting for a dryer to open up. Coin machines jammed. Socks went missing. Vern and I faced off folding sheets. He shook them hard and the corners slipped out of my hands. Vern snapped his fingers in disapproval as clean, damp linen hit dirty linoleum.

It wasn't as if we didn't care for each other; I believe we just made each other nervous. Nothing clicked. Our "special" moments included driving to the store to get Crisco®, cleaning up the storage area in the basement of our apartment, and failing to fix just about every one of our household appliances.

Forty years passed while Vern and I stayed stoic and distant. Then one night at 2:00 a.m., he called to ask for my help. Early the next morning, I flew out to Pennsylvania and brought him home to live with Sherry, me, and our dogs in Carson City. The love gates opened. Dad shared secrets that explained old family mysteries. Now in his seventies, he volunteered to help out The Change Companies®' corporate family. We watched college bowl games, swapped jokes about salesmen, and cooked brats on the grill.

Vern & Don

But Dad's heart was failing. In the months that followed, he showed me how to live through pain with courage and die with dignity. On one of his final days, we drove to a laundromat in Carson City and looked through the window. Inside, socks still went missing, but a loving relationship had been found. ■

So often we all are just looking for a little affirmation, an iota of appreciation and understanding.

▶ What a discovery! When most people ask for my advice, they really want me to just stay quiet and listen.

When friends, family members, and associates approach me, I assume they do so to tap into my experience and wisdom. I listen to their predicaments, figuring they want my point of view. The interaction will be going along just fine until I decide it's time for me to speak. Suddenly, their inquisitive faces and animated body language disappear as I begin to talk. What happened to our productive conversation?

Recently, my son, Jeff, phoned me with a question about parenting. He was concerned about his son's, my grandson's, lack of engagement in homework. I tried to listen to Jeff as he described a recent teacher's conference and the subsequent rules he planned to enforce, but I couldn't help thinking about the advice I was eager to offer.

Rather than listening to Jeff's whole story, I invested my time in shaping the delivery of my sage message. Then, when Jeff paused for a breath, I jumped in. But as I began to unfold the instructive and inspiring story of my childhood, I realized Jeff was no longer listening. In fact, I could hear him clicking through the channels on his TV.

In a remarkable number of times, more effective communication would have been achieved by the mere nodding of my head or brief responses such as "yes" or "how interesting."

Don't get me wrong, there are also times when robust exchanges are in order and rarer times when personal stories may serve a purpose.

However, so often we all are just looking for a little affirmation, an iota of appreciation and understanding.

So my tip to myself is this: "Just stay quiet and listen." ■

I realize I have just witnessed an act of love, patience, and bravery.

▶ *August 7, 1983, Cedarberg, Wisconsin*

Love, patience, and bravery, all wrapped in one dynamic old lady.

I am pulling out of my driveway when I spot a stranger on the opposite sidewalk. This stranger has a cane in one hand and a brown bag in the other. She walks with a slow gait and an indelible, wrinkled smile. She appears to be staring at Godfrey, my neighbor's oversized pit bull. Godfrey is a bit of a local nuisance. His owners are rarely home, and he barks and lunges at passersby from his patch of shade under a tree. ▶▶▶

▶ ▶ ▶ This morning, Godfrey has managed to circle around and around the tree so that his chain has secured his head against the trunk. For me, this is no big deal, and I dismiss him and the pickle he is in. On numerous occasions, Godfrey has let me know to stay out of his space, so I do. But I still pull over to the side of the street for fear the lady will do something foolish. I watch as she surveys the situation, appearing to be respectful of Godfrey's size and menacing disposition.

The lady begins to slowly walk counterclockwise around the tree, staying a foot or so out of Godfrey's reach. She's softly singing some tune, but I can't make out what language it's in. Godfrey snarls at the lady, but she patiently encourages him to retrace his circular steps, which gives him an expanding territory.

However, at about the fourth loop, she runs out of room. The neighbor's house is too close to the tree for the lady to safely escort Godfrey around without invading his space. I finally jump out from my car. This lady with the indelible smile and soft tune is going to put herself in harm's way, I tell myself.

But the lady seems to have it all figured out. She acknowledges my presence and points her cane to where she wants me to stand. She pulls out a packet of sliced bologna from her brown bag, opens it up, and hands me a slice. Her plan is to use me as a meaty decoy so that she can slip around to the other side of the house, allowing Godfrey to continue to move in the right direction.

The lady's plan works. Godfrey is free to roam his space, the lady continues her stroll down the sidewalk with her cane and brown bag, and I return to my car with my hand smelling like bologna. I realize I have just witnessed an act of love, patience, and bravery.

This is a journal entry I recently uncovered. It got me thinking: How can I be more like this old lady? Thirty years later, I'm still unwinding that one, creating more and more space for myself to cultivate those amazing skills as I go. ■

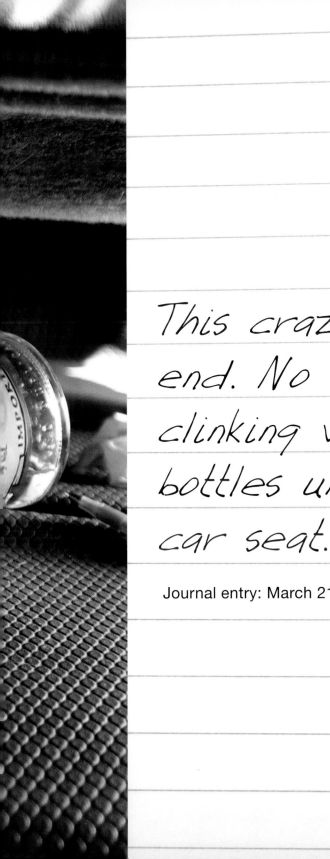

This craziness must end. No more clinking vodka bottles under the car seat.

Journal entry: March 21, 1979

▶ This journal entry didn't immediately change my life. The clinking under my car seat didn't stop the next day, or even the next year. What did develop was a daily habit of writing about my thoughts and feelings.

I journaled long before I became aware of the benefits of doing so. I was simply jotting down short bursts of emotion. I wrote about what felt good in my life, along with what didn't, and what I might do about it.

My initial journaling helped me accept professional help and move forward with my life. I learned to quit blaming others for my poor choices. In my unpolished scribblings, I uncovered creative energy, experienced joy, and rediscovered the blessings in my life that I had been wasting.

Today, my journal entries would still make little sense to others. However, looking back through them, I can map a clear path of emotional growth. Reaching decades into the past, I see how even short passages led to positive results. I inched forward, slipped back, and moved forward again. Change was, and still is, both painful and exhilarating, often at the same time. And my story is unfinished, which in and of itself is a blessing.

No matter how blind I was to the process, journaling has helped me reflect on where I've been, take stock of where I'm at, and move my life in the direction I want it to go.

I encourage myself to invest a few minutes each day to the practice. Here are some of the tried and true techniques that help unlock the power of journaling:

1. Start today – right now. Take a notebook, put the date down and write what comes to mind. Some research shows the advantages of pen and paper, but if you prefer a keyboard, go for it.

2. Don't concentrate on writing imaginatively or beautifully. Instead, let feelings, thoughts, and ideas flow.

3. Don't rethink or rewrite, just add.

4. If nothing comes to you, jot down why you think nothing is coming to you.

5. If you're looking for more structure, Google Ira Progoff or James Pennebaker, two of many experts on the benefits of writing for behavior change.

At the end of two weeks, I read my entries aloud to myself. I am always surprised to see what patterns develop. Over time, journaling even helped me bring an end to the clinking under the car seat. ■

A MAN WHO LIKES TO SOAK.

It ticks me off when self-help recovery experts use the example of a bubble bath as some kind of reward or special treat. What's more, most of the time this message is directed exclusively to women.

My bubble bath is an essential part of a full day. It is not a luxury or a reward. I do not need to earn it. I'm married to a woman who takes brief, spartan showers and humorously tries to shame me out of my chosen path to cleanliness. But I will not be intimidated by self-help authors, experts, or my spouse. I am a man who likes to soak.

It makes me think of my early days on the gridiron. Right away in grade school, I decided to be a quarterback, not for fame and glory, but because the quarterback was hit less often than other players on the football field. It amazed me that most boys acted as if they enjoyed getting slammed, or slamming others, to the ground.

Not me. If I noticed an oncoming lineman ready to flatten me as I faded back to pass, I'd rifle the ball at the back of a wide receiver who had yet to think about turning around to catch my pass. I perfected a special way of limply holding my arms up as if I were deeply troubled by the receiver's lack of effort. My football career was cut short due to my tenderness.

Okay, as long as I'm embracing self-disclosure, I enjoy watching romantic comedies, too. I laughed out loud when Harry and Sally met. I also write poetry on occasion. It certainly isn't awe-inspiring stuff, but I love pairing two original lines as if they always were meant to be together.

Over the years, I have accumulated a number of habits that diverge from the perceived masculine behavior norm. I have often deprived myself of these true pleasures in an attempt to be the person I thought alluring women and confident men wanted me to be. My age has finally freed me to embrace my true self and I've got to admit, it feels pretty good.

I have a hunch that others avoid enjoyable opportunities or play uncomfortable roles due to outside expectations. In some cases, this behavior may cause serious stress or emotional pain. It's more than just pretending to be something you're not; it's pretending to be something you don't truly want to be.

So I'll choose to keep cultivating a personal pleasure or passion that might surprise my neighbors and friends, one bubble bath at a time. ■

I'll opt to keep smiling at the cunning Mr. Quick.

▶ I recently read that cats can lower a person's blood pressure and reduce stress. I thought it was a bunch of bunk until our tabby, Roy M. Quick, entered my life.

I have four cats. Go figure! Three of them don't care a smidgen about what's going on in my life. They don't come when I call them. They stare at me from across the room until I feel uncomfortable, like I've done something wrong. They figure out where I'm walking and lay down right in front of me. In the dark. On the stairs.

Roy M. Quick is different. He comes when I call him and often when I don't. We communicate. His multi-pitched meow lets me know precisely how his day is going and he listens to me, even when I'm only thinking. He's particularly attentive at moments when I feel sad or discouraged. Roy lies on my chest, puts a paw on each side of my face, and matches the rate of his breathing to mine.

Roy is task-driven as well. He helps me shave each morning. He checks the consistency of my shaving cream and the temperature of the tap water. He makes sure I never forget the plastic cap that goes back on the blade. ▶▶▶

There's no need for an alarm clock in my life. Roy M. Quick wakes me up in the mornings (and sometimes at night) by sticking his nose in my ear. It's always invigoratingly wet and cool.

And when I'm losing to Sherry at chess or Scrabble®, with one swift swing of his tail, Roy M. Quick sends pieces flying across the table. I'm uncertain how he knows I'm losing, but I guess the odds are in his favor.

I suppose Roy's behavior could be interpreted differently. I could get annoyed with him when he loses my razor cap behind the toilet, yell at him when he wakes me in the middle of the night with a cold, wet nuzzle, or shoo him away from a close game of chess. But my blood pressure is down and I feel less stressed, so I'll opt to keep smiling at the cunning Mr. Quick. ■

▶ **Real men can fix leaking toilets. I'm a different kind of guy.** ▶ ▶ ▶

▶▶▶ Years ago, when a seldom-used toilet had been leaking for months and my in-laws were coming to visit, I knew it was time for action. I inspected the back tank and discovered that when I pulled up on the little black bobber, the leaking stopped.

Then inspiration hit. I took my third-place bowling trophy and set it down in the tank with the bowling arm strategically placed under the metal bar attached to the black bobber. The fit was perfect, the toilet was cocked for one good flush and the leaking noise was gone.

The visit was going well until my father-in-law had an upset stomach and needed to double-flush before I could sneak in to reset my contraption. It wasn't long before my "fix" for the toilet was discovered.

My bowling trophy became the family joke of the decade.

If this were a singular occurrence rather than a pattern of behavior, it would qualify as a laughably foolish incident. However, people like me have this problem with admitting we really suck at something – anything.

For a long time, I tried to hide my lack of handyman skills. I even tried to cover up this deficiency with a fancy new tool chest full of stainless steel gadgets. Unfortunately, my shortcomings became obvious once again when I couldn't open the latch on the front of the chest. I needed tools to get to my tools.

So the real problem is my willingness to accept my failings and foibles. I want to address this character flaw now by officially proclaiming to the world: **IF YOU NEED SOMETHING FIXED AROUND THE HOUSE, I'M THE WRONG GUY TO CALL.**

It feels good to have finally gone public. Now, if I can just get my family to stop laughing at me. ■

A DAY'S WORK

▶ I used to believe in the value of a hard day's work. And then I didn't. And then I did again. Beliefs are funny that way. They seem fixed, but I've realized that, through practice and patience, I can change my beliefs to get the results I want.

From an early age, my mother instilled a sense of importance, prestige, and honor in doing a job well. Sometime around my tenth birthday, she used her connections to get me a job picking up golf balls at a driving range. Early in the mornings, while it was still dark, I would walk the eight blocks to Richardson's Bowling and Golf Center and spend three hours picking up range balls. I would fill a big white bucket with them, then haul them back to the ball washing machine.

Over the next four years, I learned how to spot bowling pins, balance a cash register drawer, and drive a tractor, all as part of a job for the wonderful Mr. Richardson. I believed my job was important, and it was a privilege to receive 50 cents an hour for my work. It made me feel needed and happy. I worked diligently beyond anyone's expectations. ▶▶▶

I had reached a crossroads. My negative approach to work wasn't working.

▶ ▶ ▶ My first adult job was at a huge Reynolds Aluminum plant in McCook, Illinois, just outside of Chicago. It was a labor job on the hot-line where the ingots of glowing metal would roll down a long line to be pressed and trimmed to specification. From day one, I was told by my fellow workers to do no more than what was required. I learned to treat the foreman and the rest of the white-shirted managers who scooted around in battery-propelled carts as enemies.

I gradually changed my beliefs about work, which also changed my behavior. I began punching others' timecards, napping under scrapped sheets of aluminum foil, and committing other acts of skulduggery. I believed my job was meaningless. I felt angry. The work ethic my mother and Mr. Richardson had instilled in me was replaced by a belief that work was a hassle, a drain, and should be shortchanged in any way possible.

A few years later, I had reached a crossroads. My negative approach to work wasn't working. I realized, however, that I had a choice and soon, I decided to return to the beliefs taught by my mother and Mr. Richardson. Joy and opportunities followed. I felt back in sync with the people I respected.

We all begin picking up beliefs from the time we are babies. These beliefs influence how we feel and how we behave. Some work better for us than others. We can choose to keep our beliefs the same, or change the ones that aren't working for us quite so well.

For example, I now believe it is better to drop golf balls in a bucket with pride than it is to hide out under a scrap of aluminum foil. ■

A little frog hopped into our lives about six months ago. I believe he is taking advantage of our hospitality.

▸ When friends learn Sherry and I invest both time and dollars tending to a frog, they snicker behind our backs. But maybe life's little pleasures are worth a major investment.

A little frog hopped into our lives about six months ago. I believe he is taking advantage of our hospitality. He entered our spare garage and found his way on top of the cabinet where we accumulate tools, bolts, soiled towels, and other "handy" rubbish we never use but cannot throw away for some inexplicable reason.

Once we determined he was a long-term tenant, Sherry named him Apples. I like to think he goes to work somewhere on the garage floor during odd hours of the day, and then returns to reside atop his cabinet. After a few months, we discovered he had a few favorite spots, like behind the plastic box of unidentified nails, washers, and wing nuts, or snuggled into the crease of a faded green rag.

We extended our hospitality by filling up a little tray with dirty pond water for him. Apples climbed in immediately and stared back at us in

appreciation. Next came a box of loose black soil. Apples jumped into that as well.

When it started getting colder in the evenings, we bought Apples a warm rock that plugged into an outlet. He sat next to it, but we thought the temperature was still a little chilly so we purchased a space heater to put on the floor just below his cabinet. Next, we moved over one of our many dying houseplants so that its leaves hung over the cabinet top. Apples now has great warmth and great cover. He spends less time working on the floor and more time in his cozy residence.

Each morning before work, we check on Apples to see if he is at home. When he is, we chuckle and when he's not, we're concerned. Each evening after work, we look in on him. He's always in his pond, on his field of black dirt, or hiding back among the screwdrivers and nails. We even created an Apples song in his honor. We're pretty sure he likes it.

All this may seem insignificant and a waste of time and money. But Apples brings us joy, and joy is a commodity that makes our lives richer. ∎

OMPHAL

OSKEPSIS

▶ Belly buttons can be beautiful. Belly buttons also can become black holes.

I remember, many years ago, how self-absorbed I was regarding the significant changes I was making in my life. Every day, I would take a thorough personal inventory and share my marvelous accomplishments with the world around me. My friends and family soon grew tired of this bravado. I was looking for accolades around every corner. They were looking for me to shut up.

In the 1920s, a word was coined to describe this kind of personal reflection: omphaloskepsis. This word comes from the Greek "omphalos" (navel) and "skepsis" (examination) – in other words, navel-gazing.

A certain amount of omphaloskepsis is healthy for any individual, particularly those going through a life change. Cultivating self-awareness can lead to new perspectives, new ideas, and a new sense of personal values. At the same time, when navel-gazing becomes one's sole focus, it can create a closed cycle that actually limits personal growth.

Like everything in life, self-reflection is all about balance. During periods of significant change, a heavy dose of self-reflection is appropriate. Creating change normally requires a thorough assessment of one's past. Doing so allows healthier ways of looking at one's self and one's immediate surroundings to emerge.

So how much navel-gazing is healthy? I have found that it's different for everyone, but that part of the process of making a behavior change should involve working toward this balance. For my part, I'll continue to practice creating a healthy orbit around my belly button. I know my family and friends appreciate it. ■

So how much
navel-gazing is
healthy?

OUCH!

▶ For years, I winced at friends who shared their episodes of chronic pain with me.

I would be trying to talk about important things like how much "maple" goes into a maple bar, only to have someone interrupt about their aching feet or, worse yet, their irritable bowel syndrome. Last summer, my frustration boiled over when a neighbor asked me to turn up the volume for a pain prescription TV commercial that featured butterflies and ocean waves.

Then – ouch – my interest in chronic pain was suddenly tweaked, mainly in my neck and upper back. Now, I expect the whole world to be sensitive to my medical issue.

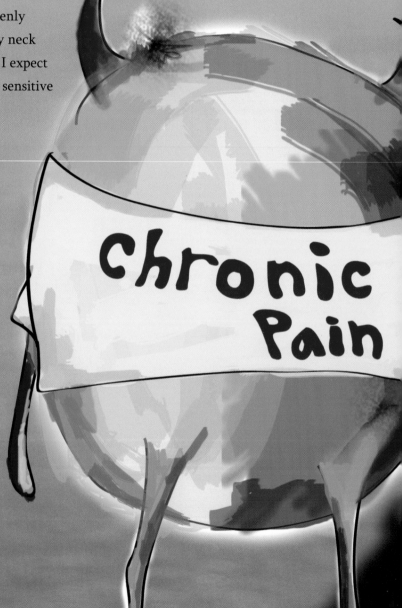

chronic Pain

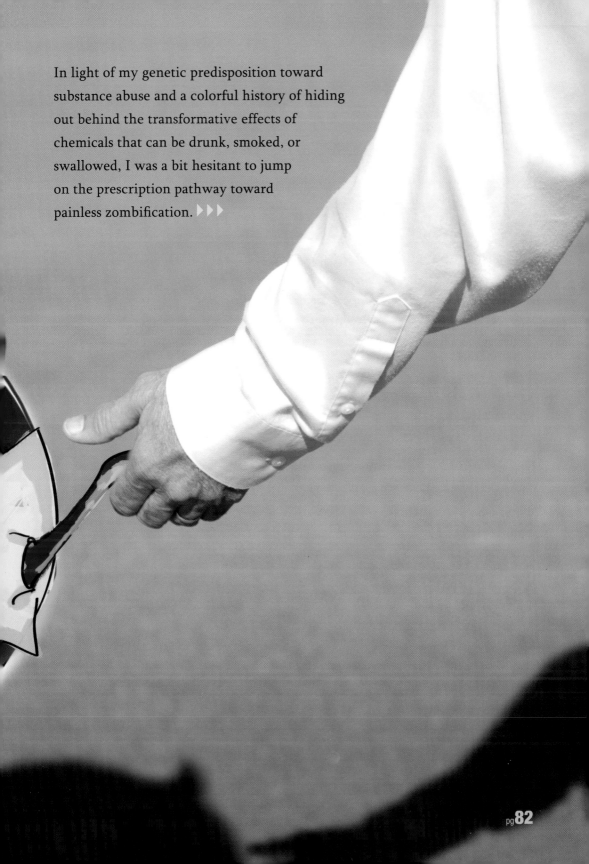

In light of my genetic predisposition toward substance abuse and a colorful history of hiding out behind the transformative effects of chemicals that can be drunk, smoked, or swallowed, I was a bit hesitant to jump on the prescription pathway toward painless zombification. ▶ ▶ ▶

▶ ▷ ▷ ▷ Plus, the advertisements, with their beautiful monarchs, idyllic pastures, and smooth-talking, white-coated actors, also stated that "other serious side effects, including death, may occur." That rapidly spoken message got me thinking about alternative routes.

My first inclination was to tough it out, be made of the right stuff, like the heroes I'd seen in the movies. It didn't take long to realize I was made of different stuff.

How about a medical procedure? I could have turned myself over to a talented surgeon for an answer. But a brief investigation on the outcome statistics of an operation, along with a discouraging conversation with my insurance representative, left me searching for another solution.

Then, I remembered a conversation I had several years ago with Steve Hayes, a gifted researcher and friend, about Acceptance and Commitment Therapy, or ACT.

From what I recalled of Steve's approach, ACT was all about noticing a situation or circumstance, accepting it, and embracing it as part of oneself. Without any more research, I decided to have a conversation with my chronic pain, invite it into my daily routine, and give it some space of its own in my life.

It's working. Now, when I go out for a walk, my self-talk says things like, "Okay pain, you can come along, but don't think you're going to lead the way." Or, as I go to bed, I say, "So, you want to hang out with me before I go to sleep? Fine, you're just giving me more time to think about the great day I'll have tomorrow."

My friends don't hear much about my spinal stenosis, but they do wonder who the heck I'm talking to. ▪

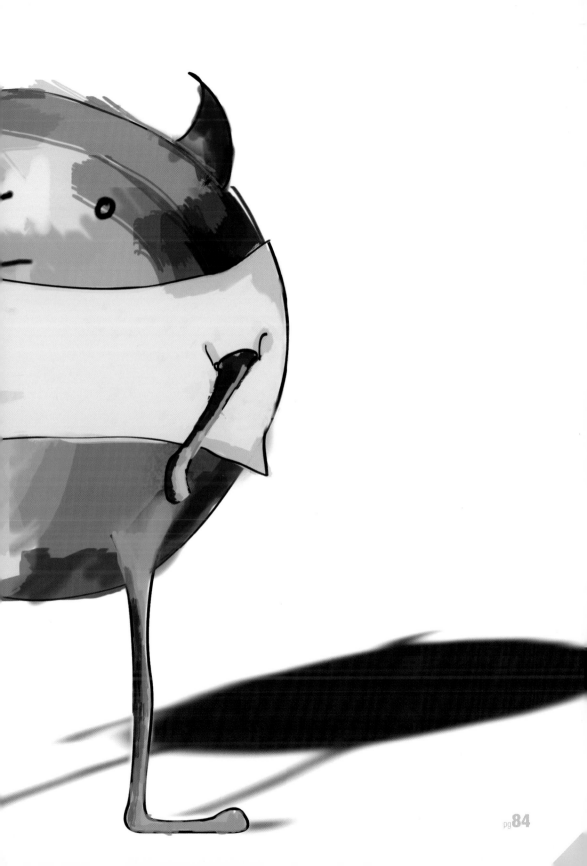

▶ Some people see their lives as something they own and maneuver the best they can. Others see themselves as victims of what life dishes up. I believe most of us have a choice in the matter.

Robbie is the adopted son of a lifelong friend. He's been through a lot. As a child, Robbie was abused in every way imaginable by people he should have been able to trust. Then, he went through a foster care system that was stretched and underfunded.

I met Robbie when he was thirteen, two years after his adoption. He was a great kid, a gifted athlete with a love of science and math. He grew tall and handsome. Robbie breezed through high school with honors in class and on the basketball court. Then college hit and something changed. Robbie left school in the second semester of his first year.

Ten years passed with a few short-lived efforts at college, several job starts, one serious run-in with the law, and lots of alcohol and drugs. Robbie's charm and intelligence got him through one calamity after another. He started treatment programs numerous times and was a patient of several psychologists. My friend, Robbie's dad, continued to try to find a solution, while his son became more depressed, then suicidal.

Eventually, Robbie came to stay with us for a while, just to rest up and gather his thoughts. He and I would walk and talk. He'd tell stories about how he had been abused as a child, about all the unadvised transitions forced on him by the foster system. He'd explain how the colleges he'd attended were totally out of sync with the modern world, and how he had been misdiagnosed by mental health professionals.

Usually, I would just listen and nod, but one day Robbie was particularly insistent. He kept pushing me for an answer.

I wanted to tell Robbie that for many years, I defined myself as a victim. I found all kinds of people and circumstances to blame for what I did or didn't do, and maybe he was stuck on the same victim path I'd traveled for so long. I wanted to tell him to get on a different path with his feelings and behavior, that taking responsibility would make him feel better.

But there was a stronger voice within me that said being quietly present was more important than providing personal stories and advice. So I stayed quiet and continued to listen.

A few days later, Robbie packed up and I haven't heard from him since.

Did I do the right thing? ■

I wanted to tell him to get on a different path with his feelings and behavior, that taking responsibility would make him feel better.

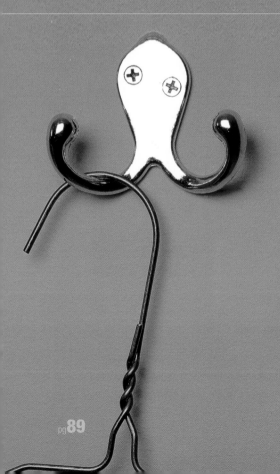

BEWARE OF
COAT HANGERS
THAT MAY
LODGE IN
YOUR NASAL
PASSAGES!

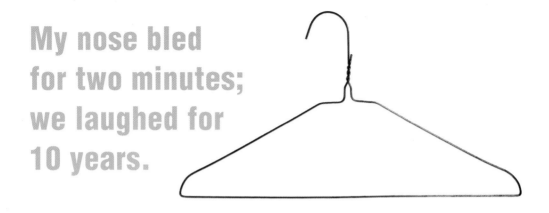

My nose bled for two minutes; we laughed for 10 years.

▶ "BEWARE OF COAT HANGERS THAT MAY LODGE IN YOUR NASAL PASSAGES!"

This sign was taped in the doorways of the Administration Building on the Washington County campus of the University of Wisconsin.

The day before, I had turned a corner and bumped into a coatrack in the hall, an impact that somehow caused a hanger to become stuck in my nose. Bob Thompson, my friend and Dean of the West Bend campus, couldn't stop laughing, despite the blood gushing from my face. He posted the warning sign, claiming he had an obligation to alert both faculty and students of such imminent danger.

My nose bled for two minutes; we laughed for 10 years.

On Saturday afternoons, Bob and I would forgo the college football games to wage a battle of our own on the driveways of suburbia. We would visit garage sales in the affluent North Side of Chicago and try to compete as barterers. Ten dollars went to whomever could uncover the tawdriest object and negotiate the asking price down by 80 percent. We'd hone our lines: "I recognize this hand-painted bumbershoot holder is worth more than your sticker says, but I already have one in a slightly different shade. Would you consider…"

We also prided ourselves on our famous Annual International Ping-Pong Tournament of Humility competition. There were always only two competitors. Thanks to a cracked ball and invisible glue I had dabbed on his side of the table, I took a 20 to 16 lead. I let Bob's next four serves bounce by me without lifting my paddle, both a gesture of brashness and love. With the score tied, Bob took a bathroom break and returned with a hanger dangling from his nose. We both had won again.

I didn't realize what a treasure Bob Thompson was until a heart condition took him away only weeks after this ping-pong game. Whenever I hang up my coat, or play a round of ping-pong, or drive by a garage sale, I silently thank Bob for his support, exuberance, and, most of all, for the laughs we shared. ◼

A PLACE IN THE PACK

▶ Kathleen Fisher, or "Catfish" for short, must be the best vet on the entire planet. She came over Friday to join Sherry and me in celebrating the life of our wonderful German shepherd, Zackery Adams. The three of us let Zack choose the spot he wanted to spend his final hour. Of course, it was under his favorite sycamore tree, which had spent many years growing up with him.

Zack had bravely endured a great amount of pain in his last few months. Getting up was a challenge and walking uphill was a tremendously courageous act. Zack's eyes asked for help. His whine was not for attention but need. We decided it was time. As Zack accepted the anesthetic from Catfish, the tense pain left his face and he was free to wander through the many memories of an abundant life.

He came to us eight years earlier as a bundle of white fur with dark, penetrating eyes. As a pup, Zack snuggled up to Sherry each night on the kitchen floor while our three large dogs waited outside for the newest member to join the pack.

Zack grew so big so fast that we passed him over to our other dogs a good month before he was emotionally ready. Like any little brother, he received the brunt of the adventures of the day, getting tumbled and nipped in the dogs' rambunctious play. Zack was a sensitive, overgrown pup, unable to defend his turf in the fashion we had come to expect from our grown dogs. He developed so many personality oddities that we affectionately called him our "DSM-IV Dog," after the *Diagnostic and Statistical Manual of Mental Disorders*, 4th edition. Zack could have kept a dog psychologist busy for an entire career. ▶ ▶ ▶

Zack's eyes asked for help. His whine was not for attention but need. We decided it was time.

▶▶▶ Zack's feelings were easily hurt. He was less quick to forgive. He developed a demanding, baritone bark that echoed throughout Washoe Valley. If his food wasn't served up right, he wouldn't eat. If you petted the other dogs before him, he would sulk. At times he was aloof, at other times, needy. He only came to you when he was good and ready and, when he did arrive, he might plow through your waiting arms with a blend of playfulness and force.

In time, Zack became good pals with our then-alpha dog, Billy Bragg. They had great battles, chasing one another into the creek, up the mountainside, and through the sagebrush and manzanita bushes. At 125 pounds, Zack was a sleek athlete who could give as good as he got. Neighbors probably thought they were at war, but Zack and Billy were, in fact, cementing the bonds of brotherly love.

And Zack became the big brother to the Rivers twins, Mike and Buddy, two shepherd puppies who received the same treatment from Zack that he remembered receiving from his older brothers in those early years. Our DSM-IV Dog had found his own form of play therapy.

Zack Adams was our grandsons' favorite dog. He made sure they could go anywhere and return safely. The crown of his head was always within finger-reach, his eyes always fixed on the road ahead. The unbridled joy between little

boys and big dogs is hard to match, and Zack became both playmate and protector to children too young to know fear.

When Catfish finally administered the lethal injection, we were ready, each of us on our stomachs with our hands reaching out to touch our beloved friend. His eyes closed and we wept, part in joy and part in knowing we were losing the affection of a good dog.

Our DSM-IV Dog had fully recovered, evolving from a scared pup into a trusted member of the pack.

And isn't that what we're all shooting for? ■

Fear

▶ Fear is my friend. I didn't always realize this, though.

Sometimes fear is self-inflicted, like when I chose to see *Psycho* as a kid. For months after that, I was afraid of shower curtains, hilltop motels, and even my dear grandmother.

Most of my early fears were not manufactured at the movie theater, though, nor could they be smothered by buttered popcorn and strips of red licorice. I remember hiding behind a bush as my school bus passed, then running the two miles to school before the bell rang. I did this because I feared the children who would be riding the bus with me. In my head, I had branded boys like Bobby Vincent and John Preston bullies because they appeared older, bolder, and more self-confident.

As an adult, I feared that I didn't measure up to anyone's expectations. I was terrified that others were paying special attention to me, waiting for me to mess up in one way or another. Because of this self-imposed fear, I was always looking to do the unusual, the spectacular, to prove my worth. Sometimes I'd make up accomplishments or personality traits to meet these imaginary expectations. Other times, I would abuse alcohol to get by. Of course, such actions only intensified my fear.

Even though I didn't know it at the time, fear was my friend. It had its way of setting off alarms in my head and forcing me to confront my false beliefs and behaviors. By paying attention to my fear and what it was telling me, I realized that my adult fears turned out to be the same as they were in my school bus days. I recognized that I am not the center of anyone else's world, which helped me take the next small step away from fear and toward the life I wanted to live. Paying attention to my fear brought my feelings into check and gave me the freedom to appreciate myself and others.

Psycho and other scary movies pale in comparison to the scenarios we can orchestrate in our own minds. It's comforting to know we have the power to direct our own scripts and endings. ■

I recognized that I am not
the center of anyone else's
world, which helped me take
the next small step away from
fear and toward the life I
wanted to live.

Fear

▶ **If you think you know about all of the things your kids did growing up, think again.** ▶ ▶ ▶

▶ ▶ ▶ I thought my daughter, Kate, was the perfect child. She was valedictorian of her high school. She was undefeated on her tennis team. She won state debate tournaments, graduated from Northwestern University, and landed a job with Paramount Studios, where her first assignment was marketing the motion picture *Forrest Gump*.

I could have easily gone on with this utopian view of my daughter, but recently over dinner, some childhood truths were revealed.

When Jeff, my son and Kate's older brother, was nine, he broke a prized antique rocking chair while Kate was doing her homework at the kitchen table. Unlike his sister, Jeff had a flair for creative mischief. He attempted to cover up the damaged chair by wrapping the broken leg with adhesive tape and using a black crayon to match the color. The ruse was quickly discovered, and I lined up Jeff and Kate for questioning. Jeff admitted total guilt, saving his little sister from any unfair punishment.

But as it was revealed to me, the real story went like this: Kate and Jeff were playing make-believe, and Kate wanted him to be an elephant. She put the antique rocking chair on his back and climbed aboard, the queen of some ancient country. As this fantasy queen looked over her realm (the living room), the chair leg she was standing on broke. The quick-thinking queen then offered to pay Jeff a week's allowance if he took the blame and resulting consequences. ▶ ▶ ▶

▶ ▶ ▶ This turned out to be the same "perfect daughter" who, for years, unwrapped and then rewrapped every gift for Jeff and herself that was under the Christmas tree. Kate received a small "allowance bonus" from Jeff for her meticulous skill set. Days before Christmas morning, they would practice with each other looks of surprise and pleasure as they opened their presents in front of their parents.

The bottom line is that both Jeff and Kate grew up to be responsible, caring parents. Now, they stroll around thinking they know every detail of their kids' activities. As Grandpa, I know better. ■

▶ Dennis Beckman is a mentor, friend, and the best listener I have ever had the privilege to talk to.

Dennis invests his whole self into understanding what any person tells him. I've watched him carefully. It's a thing of beauty.

He doesn't finish a sentence or thought for another person. He doesn't start nodding his head before the other person is done. His whole body is focused on the speaker, not in an intrusive, "I can't wait until you are finished" way, but in an interested, "Isn't that fascinating" manner.

Dennis also has a habit of letting a second or two pass after a person is done speaking. He doesn't jump into the open space but lets the speaker's last words linger. I've never heard him try to one-up a person's story or summarize what someone said that doesn't need summarizing. Because of his listening skills, most people think Dennis is really smart.

Last year, I watched Dennis apply his listening art to a very angry couple who believed their preteen daughter had been mistreated at a soccer tournament. As a volunteer referee, Dennis had just finished the second of three games under a sweltering summer sun. The father ranted and the mother shook her fist, but Dennis just listened. He hadn't even made the call in question, yet he wanted to understand the parents' reasoning and provide a sounding board for their frustration.

When the parents were depleted and they had time to take a few breaths, Dennis told them that he knew the refs accidentally blew calls in almost every game and apologized for this circumstance. He also offered to talk to the daughter. The parents declined, retreating to their air-conditioned car and very embarrassed daughter. Dennis returned to the field for his third game.

The difference between Dennis and me is that his actions were heartfelt and solution-focused. I'd still be preaching to those parents – that is, if I had ever let them voice their frustrations in the first place. ■

BROOM CLOSET

▶ He felt lonely, desperate, and afraid. It was 6:30 in the morning and he had collapsed in the broom closet of his tiny office. Sweaty and awake since four, he had already consumed a quart of vodka to prepare for the consequences of another day. He squeezed his eyes shut against all light and tried to block out the smell of vomit that soured his clothes.

This young man had long harbored dreams of success, but reality was starting to sink in. He was deeply in debt to dangerous people, reliably drunk by noon every day, and had just forged a batch of financial documents. He had been fighting his personal demons for a long time.

He heard the outer door of the office open and a single set of footsteps walk toward the closet. There was the sound of a hand on the door handle and the closet door opened. The young man closed his eyes even tighter. His body began to shake.

After several agonizing seconds of silence, the closet door eased shut and the unknown visitor retreated from the office.

From that moment forward, the young man decided to quit hiding from himself. He sought professional help and began to face the consequences of his actions.

Some people might define this moment as "hitting bottom." Others might call it a spiritual awakening or moment of personal insight. Behavior change is a lifelong process, but personal moments of awakening are sometimes all it takes to start a period of positive change.

I will always be grateful for that gentle hand opening a door. ■

▶ When it comes to anxiety, I like the analogy that many of us behave like a bunch of ducks in a pond. We attempt to appear calm, confident, and peaceful above the water while our webbed feet are going like crazy under the surface. ▶ ▶ ▶

▶ ▶ ▶ Henry David Thoreau wrote that most men lead lives of quiet desperation. He must have spotted a duck or two at Walden Pond.

What got me thinking about anxiety was partly a National Public Radio program I heard recently, and my own experience as I tuned in. I caught the first bit of this program in the car on the way to work. As I pulled into the company's parking lot, I listened to a PhD-ed author talk about anxiety as a fear of fear, but I was quickly distracted. A group of fellow employees came out the front door of our office building, talking and laughing as they made their way toward their cars.

I was sure they were looking at me sitting there in my car, and probably even talking about what an odd bird I was for lurking in the lot. I decided to hop out and wave them down to explain my behavior, but I surprised them. They didn't even know I was sitting there. I returned to my car in even more of a kerfuffle than before, just in time to miss the end of the program on anxiety.

As is true with most essentials of a happy, productive life, anxiety is an emotion that works best when in balance. Anxiety can be a good thing. It drives us forward, moving us out of a state of complacency or boredom. Yet, too much anxiety can freeze us up, making us worry about what's coming next. Healthy anxiety keeps us in the present moment, alert to the many possibilities in front of us. Unhealthy anxiety drags us into the unknowable future.

I love Woody Allen movies for this reason. He's so good at playing a person who's made a mess of his surroundings. He acts out angst and second-guessing perfectly, yet manages to make it funny at the same time. When we laugh at the characters he plays, we have an opportunity to laugh at ourselves. And that may give us a better remedy for unhealthy anxiety than any duck or PhD expert can serve up. ■

MEANIES

▶ Over the years, I've gotten chewed out by teachers, bosses, coaches, and friends – and I'd like to thank each one of them. ▶ ▶ ▶

▶ ▶ ▶ Although I thought of them as meanies at the time, I realize now that these people cared enough about me to put me in my place. Such critical advice seems less common today. Still, I hate to think where I'd be if everyone had tried to make me feel good about my screwups or told me I was well above average when, in reality, my lackadaisical attitude made me mediocre at best.

Here's a small sampling of thank yous to those caring meanies:

Thanks, Mrs. Fillmore, for telling me I was way behind in high school chemistry class. Thank you for telling me it was totally my fault, not yours, because most everyone else in class was doing fine. Your hunch was that I was smart enough, just unmotivated. I particularly appreciate how you said all of this in front of my parents and then later repeated it in front of the entire class. I passed with a solid C.

A special thank you goes out to Coach Bub Collins, who had me stay after basketball practice to let me know I would not make the team. Remember, Coach, how you put your arm around my shoulder and told me matter-of-factly that I was slower than most of my teammates, I couldn't jump, and I shot too much? At the time, I thought I was star material, but you were right on all fronts.

To my friend, Larry Case: thank you for yelling at me in college for throwing candy wrappers out the car window and skipping most of my classes. You liked me. You wanted me to stay in school and not mess up the environment. I quit throwing candy wrappers out the window, but I flunked out of college. (You can't get everything right the first time.)

I also want to thank my boss, Rueben, for writing me a detailed note letting me know I was fired. You made a list of things I was supposed to do that I hadn't, and a whole separate list of things I did do that I shouldn't have. You also followed up with a phone call loudly emphasizing the same message. I did a lot more of what I was supposed to do on my next job.

I could go on and on thanking the people in my life who delivered robust and honest dialogue. Many of these same people also boosted my self-esteem and congratulated me for good work when I had earned it. A few inspired me by painting pictures of the person I could become. When it comes right down to it, though, so much of my ability to accept and adapt to what's in front of me each day comes from those caring meanies who insisted on telling me the unfiltered truth. ∎

▶ I've never had high expectations for teenagers with fluorescent hair and facial piercings. I have no idea where this stereotype comes from, but it has definitely influenced my thoughts and behaviors over the years.

It's strange, then, when an experience comes along that totally shatters what I've been telling myself.

So I'm in a cheap rental car outside of Denver when my cell phone slides off my car seat and lodges itself among the metal braces below. I pull into a minimart parking lot to retrieve it. It's cold and I'm running late. With my legs sticking out the door, I reach down between the seats to find my thin, do-it-all device.

My hand gets stuck. It hurts. The more I pull, the stucker I get. I hear people passing, muffled laughter. I'm too embarrassed to call out.

"Let's get you out of there."

I look up and see a lanky girl with bright pink hair and metal rings attached to her nose, lips, and eyebrows. She kneels next to me. She cups one of her hands over my stuck one. With her other hand, she moves the car seat lever back slowly. I'm free.

The ringed rescuer is not done. She asks for my phone number, calls it on her phone, and we both hear the silly tune playing on my cell. Using her thin and very tattooed arm, the girl retrieves my lost object.

My stereotype is totally busted. Based on appearance only, this young lady is the last person I would have bet on saving my hand and my dignity.

I want to give her 20 dollars as a thank-you tip, but she refuses. "My pleasure," she says. "You'd do the same for me."

I hope she's right. ■

My stereotype is totally busted.

How can a modern
clothes dryer compare
to such a memory?

▶ What brings you joy?

Sherry, President of The Change Companies®, speaks fondly of drying clothes on a clothesline with her Aunt Janie. Sherry would hand her two clothespins at a time and Aunt Janie would pin the sheets, work shirts, and other freshly washed items against the blue Oklahoma sky. The sunshine and the westerly winds would do the work, and the soft flapping of the drying clothes provided a peaceful backdrop to conversations about puppies, pancakes, and other summer delights.

How can a modern clothes dryer compare to such a memory?

I sometimes wonder if today's cutting-edge technologies are disrupting the little pleasures that define the joy of life. There are a lot of benefits to car navigation systems, but I miss giving directions to lost motorists that include white picket fences and old red barns.

Right before I go to sleep, I sometimes think of what makes me feel whole and happy. I conclude that it's the same things that I enjoyed when I was ten: throwing and catching a football, reading a good short story, or gently rubbing the ears of a sleepy dog. This isn't to say that all great things are buried in the past, but perhaps we assume that progress always brings joy. We trade something precious for something faster, slicker, or easier.

What little things inspire joy in your life? Are there places or smells or activities that bring a quiet glow of serenity to the rush of your day? You might be surprised at the happiness some of these simple pleasures still contain.

And if your car's navigation system ever takes you through Washoe Valley on Old Highway 395, don't be surprised to see the billows of Sherry's shirts and sheets hanging out to dry. ■

▶ I'm late and agitated. The Reno streets are packed with Christmas shoppers who drive as if visions of sugarplums are dancing in their heads. The right lane of Virginia Street is decorated with those orange detour cones that limit traffic to a single lane. Two green lights come and go and now it's my turn to bust out of the jam.

But the lady in front of me waves four cars coming out of the parking lot to go in front of her. Who designated her as the representative of all the drivers stuck behind her? She clears out the parking lot, but our row is stymied. Another red light. I'm furious. I want to jump out of my car and swing a gift-wrapped golf putter through her windshield.

My next stop is the grocery store. I'm standing behind a shopper who decides not to reach for his wallet until his groceries are bagged and the total is presented, like: Surprise! Now he needs to figure out which card to use, and which way to slide it. But before he can even do that, he starts discussing with the checker the various ways to determine the freshness of asparagus. Just what I need right now: a vegetable-savvy conversationalist. ▶ ▶ ▶

Decaf

Shots

Syrup

Milk

DAWN

...ing you're about to enjoy is extremely hot.
...50% post-consumer recycled fibre

"Have an extra-fun day!"

▶▶▶ I experience similar frustrations whenever I'm at the airport. Why don't the people jammed in front of me walk down the steps of the escalator? Why do they stand there like it's some Disneyland ride to be cherished for as long as possible? And why can't the escalator itself move any faster? Do people expect this agonizingly slow descent to be some highlight after a week of travel?

This agitated and frustrated me is one of the me's I deal with on a regular basis. What's saddest of all is I have plenty of time on my hands. In all of these situations, I'm not rushing about saving the world. At best, I'm on my way home to pick up the dog poop in the backyard.

Fortunately, I also recognize people are capable of changing the way they feel and behave. So I decide this is one aspect of my personality I wish to reshape, for my own good and the good of those around me.

I know the perfect place to practice patience and social bantering is my local Starbucks shop. I enter to find people smiling, calling each other by their first names, and eagerly waiting in line to describe in detail the exact syrups and toppings to add to their grande coffees. I watch one happy barista printing precise instructions on each cup and then passing it on to the next several happy baristas who grind, whip, and concoct each order, all while smiling customers wait for their names to be called.

When it is my turn, I order a "small black coffee, extra hot, for Don." I practice waiting with patience for my name to be announced.

And I make a promise to myself: whenever my name is finally called, I will sashay forward, accept the cup that says "DAWN," and when I'm told to have an "extra-fun day," that's exactly what I will have. ■

Since dogs romp through life at a seven-to-one year ratio to humans, there are many lessons they can teach us about our thoughts and behaviors. This is the story of Billy Bragg, our alpha German shepherd. For eight years, he roamed the Sierra Nevada mountain range with Sherry, me, and the rest of our dogs.

Even as a pup, Billy liked to separate from the pack and gallop after low-flying eagles. I always wondered if he was trying to chase them or join them. (Message for humans: There is a joy in pursuing lofty goals, even if those around you think you are a bit nuts.)

Billy Bragg never learned how to give dog kisses. Instead, he showed his love for Sherry and me by nipping at our faces, particularly our noses. Facial nicks became a status symbol in our home. (Message for humans: Love is shown in many ways. Be open to accepting unconditional love, even if it smarts from time to time.)

Billy Bragg received no training and knew no tricks. And yet, throughout his adulthood, he led as alpha dog with a natural and flawless confidence. (Message for humans: People will respond more to your behaviors than your rules or stated expectations.)

Whenever our other three shepherds ran toward the front fence to scuffle with our neighbor's dogs, Billy Bragg would cut them off at the pass and assertively steer them back to the house. (Message for humans: Prompt action can avert serious problems. Leaders rush to the fire.)

Late one night, a black bear entered our home through the living room window. Fortunately, Billy was there. He gave a growl so frightful that the bear jumped right back through the window and scampered up the mountainside. (Message for humans: Friends come to the rescue, even during dangerous times.)

The day before Billy Bragg yielded to a fast-moving cancer, he joined us for a joyous winner's lap around his mountainous property. He led the pack as he always had, with authority and dignity. (Message for humans: Live your life to the fullest, finish your responsibilities, and continue to love until the end.)

Often, as we continue to hike with our three German shepherds up Billy Bragg's mountain, a single eagle flies low against the deep blue sky. (Message for humans: The spirit of life continues with the pack we leave behind.)

BILLY BRAGG,
THE PUP

BILLY BRAGG, THE ALPHA

The spirit of life continues with the pack we leave behind.

ADVENTURE

THE ADVENTURE

CONTINUES...

▶ I've done my best to learn from the life events and little choices I've experienced over time. I've worked to make changes where I could, and when I couldn't do it alone, I relied on the support of family members, mentors, friends, and, yes, even alter egos.

Binder-Man sometimes visits me in my dreams. Together, we pour over memories like pages of a photo album, or, perhaps more appropriately, a comic book series. We flip past stories of me as a child, a teenager, a young adult, and onward. There are disturbing images in there that are still difficult to look upon, and other scenes that show serenity and joy. I used to think of Don Kuhl as Binder-Man's mild-mannered counterpart, but looking back through these pages, I start to wonder if maybe it's the other way around. ▶▶▶

▶▶▶ This is what I've come to believe: I'm a fortunate fellow. I have created a lifelong adventure series rich in content and color. And like a true first-edition, it gets better with age. I can recognize the importance of revisiting these stories from time to time, and relearning the lessons they contain. And those disturbing scenes that give me the creeps? They are a part of who I am; they provide a truthful contrast so I can better appreciate the total me.

The exploits of Binder-Man are far from over. More of my adventure series may lie behind me than ahead, but I am working to approach each day, each minute, each action-packed frame with a caped-crusading attitude. The support of Binder-Man and many others have bound the pages of my life together, both good and bad. And I find great joy in knowing I'm the one who determines what goes into the remaining frames. ■

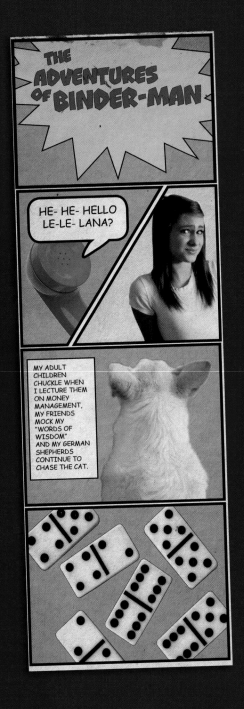

APPLES

Vern & Don

OUCH!

ANXIETY

AT ONE TIME OR ANOTHER, ALL OF US HAVE BEEN IN THE MIDST OF FACING THE CONSEQUENCES OF OUR BEHAVIORS.

Scott Provence has an MA in English and an MFA in Creative Writing from the University of Washington. A native of Seattle, Scott enjoys demonstrating the many applications of an English degree, which so far have included everything from teaching college courses to performing in halftime shows for the NBA.

With a bachelor's degree in Digital New Media and Design from New York University, **Jennifer Sande** joined The Change Companies® in 2011 to aid in the production of print materials, become a social media guru, and lend her skills as a photographer when needed (which is often).

Johanna Landis earned her BA and MA in English from Western Washington University, and is currently working toward a PhD in the Literature and Environment Program at the University of Nevada, Reno. When she's not reading, writing, or discussing ideas, she's probably playing with her cats, finding ways to get lost in nature, or planning her next trip to Disneyland.

Don Kuhl. Enough about me.

Holly Moxley is an artist and creative thinker, happiest when she can work through a challenge and come out on the other side with effective and beautiful results.

THE CHANGE COMPANIES®

This is a book about behavior change. The experiences shared here may be personal, but they also have shaped the history of a thriving organization. For over 24 years, The Change Companies® has worked to empower individuals to make positive life changes. The brief stories told by its founder, Don Kuhl, serve as vehicles for a larger change movement The Change Companies® represents, one that has touched the lives of over 20 million individuals.

This is a simple book, because making life changes can also be simple. It all begins with the little choices made each day. The Change Companies® has learned from great researchers and practitioners how we are in charge of our own lives. We are our own leading experts. The way we think, feel, and act is within our control.

Although professional caregivers, friends, and family can provide significant assistance in helping us through challenging times, the joy and contributions we share throughout our lives are up to us to put into play. The Change Companies® hopes readers will find not only joy in these brief vignettes, but also material for applying a few of the evidence-based solutions for leading healthy, productive lives.

If parts of this book resonate with you, you may wish to learn more about The Change Companies® at changecompanies.net. Or give us a call at 888-889-8866. Better yet, swing by Carson City, Nevada, and visit our dedicated group of changing individuals. Don and the rest of The Change Companies®' family look forward to hearing from you.

These stories of Don's (and more) appear every Wednesday in his blog, Mindful Midweek. To subscribe to these thoughtful midweek reflections, visit www.changecompanies.net/subscribe